Sunf

Story by Joy Cowley
Photographs by Sarah Irvine

I put a sunflower seed
in my garden.

Down came the sunshine.

Down came the rain.

Up came a little shoot.

It grew, and it grew,
and it grew.

Out came my sunflower,
my big, yellow sunflower.

7

My sunflower grew old.
Now I have lots
of sunflower seeds.